CREDO

MEDITATIONS ON THE APOSTLES' CREED

CREDO

MEDITATIONS
ON THE
APOSTLES' CREED

HANS URS VON BALTHASAR

INTRODUCTION BY MEDARD KEHL, S.J.

TRANSLATED BY DAVID KIPP

IGNATIUS PRESS   SAN FRANCISCO

Original German edition:
Credo; Meditationen turn Apostolischen Glaubensbekenntnis
© 1989 by Verlag Herder, Freiburg im Breisgau

Cover art: Christ and the Apostles
Early Christian fresco, Catacomb of S. Domitilla, Rome, Italy
© Scala / Art Resource, New York

Cover design by Roxanne Mei Lum

Published by Ignatius Press 2000, 2005, 2014

ISBN 978-0-89870-803-5
ISBN 978-1-68149-118-9 (eBook)
Library of Congress Control Number 00-100817

Printed in the United States of America ∞

CONTENTS

INTRODUCTION

In 1988, over a period of twelve months, the pastoral bulletin for the German dioceses of Aachen, Berlin, Essen, Hildesheim, Koln, and Osnabriick published, each month as its leading article, one then another of some brief interpretations of the twelve "articles" of the Apostles' Creed that were written by the Swiss theologian, Hans Urs von Balthasar. Although he himself may not, perhaps, have conceived them as such when writing them, these texts, which are undoubtedly among the last things to be written by him, nevertheless take on the character of a legacy in view of his sudden death on 26 June 1988. For they amount, in their extraordinary compactness and depth, to a little "summa" of his theology. What he has set out in detail, over five decades, in the now barely surveyable manifoldness and breadth of his truly "catholic" thought—that is, thought that draws its sustenance from the inexhaustible fullness of the self-revelation of God and thus transcends all confessional narrowness—he summarizes once again here in contemplative plainness and simplicity.

After having tirelessly pursued the many pathways and tracks, however winding, of the incarnate love of God in our world, he now returns, at the end, to that center of our reality from which all things spring: to the Mystery of the threefold God. The astonished, grateful gaze of one who, out of adoration for this Mystery, knows himself called to theological thought and research remained with him to the end; never was he simply "finished" with the "subject matter" of his theology, never was he able to

7

finalize documentation of a theological system based on it, never did his "looking" become a knowing, self-comforted "seeing through." Precisely this unclouded, almost childlike joy in the richness and beauty of that Mystery which entices and attracts our faith constantly anew is evidenced in his interpretation of the creed. My comments in this introduction are aimed at directing the reader's attention primarily to *the* characteristic feature of those meditations, namely, to:

The Trinitarian stamp of faith. The preeminent value of this exposition of the creed, which sets it apart from other similar attempts, lies in the consistently reasoned and inter-balanced way in which von Balthasar brings out the trinitarian structure of the Christian faith, both as a whole and as unfolded in the twelve "articles of faith." The "sign of the Cross," which, from baptism onward, brings the believer's entire life under the name and benediction of the threefold God, thus also stands, from the very start, as a foretoken of his explicit profession of faith in this God, a foretoken that illuminates not only the inner unity of the three-part profession, but also the deepest meaning of each individual statement of faith. Without lengthy introductions and guiding commentaries, without much seeking after understandable "links" to the sphere of faith's natural experience, von Balthasar moves immediately into the center: that Christian faith is nothing other than allowing oneself to receive what is bestowed by that God "who, in his essence, is love and surrender" (29).

"In his essence": This means that God does not need the finite world before he can be love and surrender, but is always such in his very self: an inexhaustible relational process of reciprocal self-surrender between Father, Son, and Spirit. The unity of this God is not, therefore, the unity of a consciousness and will related purely to itself, nor the unity of some natural, cosmic life-force, but the unity of love; and in fact, understood as a (supratemporal) process involving an original source of love that bestows itself infinitely ("Father"), a self-declaration of love that receives and gives itself back infinitely ("Son"), and a love that binds together infinitely, bringing giving and receiving into accord and effecting their overflow into creation infinitely ("Spirit"). To render the history of redemption transparent in relation to this primal process is probably the deepest concern of the whole of von Balthasar's theology. This can also be easily demonstrated by the particular steps in his interpretation.

It begins with the matter of correctly understanding "God the Father *Almighty*": his "almightiness" lies not (as often imagined by us) in "being able to do this or that as he chooses," but in the unlimited and free power of his surrender, which can bring forth "an Other in God," namely, the Son as a counterpart who is equally essential and equal in love and power (31). In the Holy Spirit—the personal fruit of this love—God's "almightiness" transcends itself in the direction of creation, which therefore owes its being entirely to the effect of the threefold God. Its *meaning*, after all, lies solely in the mutual glorification of Father and Son in the common Spirit of love (32), and its *being made possible* solely in that "Other," who lives in God himself and consequently affords both scope and "surety" for the successful out-come of the created other (39). The world can be created only "in the Son," who is thus—precisely in view of the possibility and actuality of the world's no to the Creator—also simultaneously the "guarantor for the success of the venture" (39). In full freedom—having, as it were, been granted permission to accept the Father's request—the Son assumes, from eternity, his "destiny" as mediator, archetype, and savior of creation (39–40) in order to carry it out, historically, in the *Incarnation* and, in the sanctifying power of the Spirit, to draw all creatures into his unique relationship with the Father. Only in that way can we join in his gratitude (*eucharistia*) and supplication and be entitled to pray the "Our Father."

Here, a further theme of the interpretation, which can be illuminated only in *trinitarian* terms, announces itself: the Son's *obedience*. This by no means stands in contradiction to his freedom and love, for in obedience the Son's inner-trinitarian essence expresses itself in an appropriately creaturely way. As love that continually receives itself from the Father and owes itself to him, he also always accepts, with "full consent," his being sent to the world, and allows himself to undergo his passive "conception" by the Holy Spirit and his birth of the Virgin Mary (45). Freely assenting obedience, as the form of creaturely freedom and love that is appropriate to the eternal Son, will thenceforth stamp the whole path of the earthly Jesus and of those who follow after him.

Thus it is no wonder that the creed moves directly from the birth of Jesus to his Passion; for at the "hour" of his suffering, perishing, and descent into the realm of death, there is demonstrated for the first time, through his obedience, the deepest power of God's love, a power which really changes and heals *everything*. Here, once again in freely willed assent, the Son takes upon himself the entire "burden of the world's guilt"—that is, the radical remoteness from God and the forlornness caused by us sinners—suffers it through in himself and thus brings God's merciful love even to precisely those who are (in the theological sense) "dead," namely, those who banish themselves from God and shut themselves up in their loneliness. "Died a death in final companionship with all sinners, but a dark death; for which night is darker than the one that the forlorn God has known most intimately?" (53).

This inner correspondence between the Trinity and obedience, which allows the obedience of Jesus, and also—through conferred participation—of those who follow after him, to become, as it were, *the* sacrament of God's love in our history, is clarified by von Balthasar in a further step pertaining to belief that the Lord has risen, has ascended, and will come again. It is the triune God who effects the Resurrection of Jesus in the almightiness of the Father's life-giving love, in the mediation of this love to creation by the Spirit (cf. Rom 8:11), and in a receptivity to this love on the part of the Son that extends all the way to the ultimate emptiness of death. Thus death, as a manifestation of sinful remoteness from God, is finally overcome forever, indeed, even more: In the form of the loving, obedient self-surrender of Jesus, death's actual meaning in the context of creation reveals itself, namely, its being a radical image of original life, which is nothing other than that living process of reciprocal self-surrender between Father, Son, and Spirit (59). Into this reconciliation between life and death—so we may hope—our own death, no matter how paltry, will also be taken up and overcome.

Jesus' return, replete with the "harvest of the world," "to the starting point of his mission" (63), that is, to the Father, carries with it the promise that the whole of created reality will also be granted participation—on the universal plane—in, his life. It is toward this that the present, inner-historical activity of the Son of Man is directed, precisely in his struggle against the ungodly powers; and this is also what is primarily served by the *judgment* of the world that the Father has assigned to the Son. With this judgment, he grants to him, the Son of Man, who has experienced and knows everything human from the inside, a share in his world-perfecting almightiness. This is why, too, the power of God's corrective love shows itself precisely in an attraction to the good that moves, but does not overpower, our hearts. Nobody knows in advance whether any particular person can really resist to the end the enticement and courtship of that love. But whoever also dares, "in fear and hope," to "throw himself blindly into the arms" of the Lord can certainly hope to gain nothing but the opposite, for self and for everyone. And indeed, this is so precisely in view of the sole decisive criterion for that judgment, namely, the mercifulness that is asked of us (cf. Mt 18:33; Jas 2:13) and that we may therefore also expect, in hope, on the part of our Judge (71).

The third major section of the creed begins with the declaration of belief in the *Holy Spirit*. Once again von Balthasar explicates the special role played, this time by the Spirit, in the trinitarian and redemptive process of God's love. He does so in a very careful and reserved manner, for he is conscious of dealing here with the "most mysterious aspect of God," which can "never be captured in rigid concepts" (75). The Spirit's nature is left suspended in this barely comprehensible dialectic: Being an "Other" in God who is different, in turn, from both Father and Son, namely, as the personal "result" of their unity and "communio," yet, at the same time, as a "pregiving" of their love that is common to both and out of which the Father gives himself to the Son and the Son gives himself back to the Father; for God is, in any case, always the Spirit of love and surrender. Eastern and Western understandings of the Spirit could meet with each other in this interpretation. In the context of redemptive history, the significance of the Holy Spirit lies in his working within our spirit (not repressing but liberating it) and disclosing to us the Mystery of God. "To him, the most delicate, vulnerable, and precious one in God, we must open ourselves up, without defensiveness, without thinking that we know better, without hardening ourselves, so that we may undergo initiation by him into the Mystery that God is love" (76).

Also regarding the last four articles of faith, which acknowledge the redemptive work of the threefold God, von Balthasar adheres consistently to his interpretive principle: Through the Eucharist of the Son and the mission of the Spirit, the *Church*—which is rooted in the choosing of Israel by Yahweh ("a name of God that is still only on its way to the Father of Christ," 37)—is molded into a shape appropriately respondent to God's love, that is, into the body and the bride of Christ. To that extent, we can recognize in her "a structural image of the threefold God that brings creation to completion" (84). As "holy" and "catholic," she extends the redeeming movement of God out into the entire world; as (eucharistic) "communion of saints," in which no one any longer lives and dies for self alone (cf. 2 Cor 5:14), she can rightly be both image and symbol of the reciprocal self-sharing that is inherent in the threefold life of God.

The "forgiveness of sins," which the Church mediates mainly through baptism and confession, is granted to us by the Father, at the request of the Son, through the Holy Spirit, who opens our closed hearts to God's love and thus makes it possible that we ourselves forgive one another's guilt in order to live in reconciliation with God and with each other.

When dealing with the closing phrase of the creed, which speaks of the Christian's hope for "*life everlasting*," von Balthasar's interpretation undoubtedly reaches its high point. Even in the language alone, the words acquire a tone that sweeps one along and arouses enthusiasm, as if spoken by someone who sees his passage into this eternal life as a prospect immediately before him and, in his irrepressible joy, would like to infect those many others, who drag themselves so wearily through this present life and yearn for nothing more than "eternal peace," with his youthfully forward-pressing hunger for living. Thus, in von Balthasar's trinitarian perspective, "eternity" and "life" lose their colorless, well-worn meanings; they suddenly become filled with symbols of love and its gladdening, inventive play of giving and thanking and uniting. Here, there is talk of unimagined surprises and adventures, of constantly new departures and excursions; here, the eighty-three-year-old does not grow tired of praising the unfathomable miracle—never endangered by boredom, stagnation, or cessation—of eternal communion with God and his saints. Even the sufferings of our times will reveal, in the end, their meaning that was hidden in God's love: "And if we are given to suffer, deeper shafts are sunk in us than we thought we could contain, depths destined to become, in the life everlasting, reservoirs of greater happiness, wells still more productive. Wells that flow forth of themselves, gratis, for in the life everlasting, all is gratis" (103).

OTHER POSITIONAL OPTIONS. Along with this fundamental, trinitarian interpretative principle, two other positional options can be recognized in his interpretation of the creed which—precisely in their apparent contrariety—have always given von Balthasar's theology its characteristic profile:

Meditation on the Word. Anyone familiar with von Balthasar's theological work will be struck, when reading these texts, by how little the author draws, in this case, on the richly filled treasure-houses of his literary, historical, philosophical, and theological knowledge. Almost exclusively, a single book is cited: Holy Scripture, the original document of our faith. Use of this methodological and stylistic device indicates how much von Balthasar is concerned with a final stopping in at, and turning back to, the original center of redemptive history. All embellishing, descriptive, and elaborative "augmentation" can now be dispensed with. When a man sets about committing his lifework back into the hands of the one from whom he has received everything, the "original sound" of God's Word is enough for him.

Listening meditatively to this Word alone, and "turning it over and over" in his mind, was learnt by von Balthasar from the great saints, above all, from Mary, the archetype of the Church and of each individual believer within her. To undergo molding into the "form" of her faith—which enabled her to "keep all these words in her heart" (cf. Lk 2:19, 51) and to "let it be" to her in accordance with the word (Lk 1:38)—was something that von Balthasar allowed himself more and more unreservedly, all the way to the point of this final "concentration" on Holy Scripture. Thus this little book serves as yet another beautiful testimony to the fundamentally Marian approach of his theology and spirituality. It is probably here, too, that the deepest explanation for his unerring analytical power is to be found, a power which, in recent years, he has brought to bear again and again in debates about the specific nature of Christian meditation. For him, all the many different methods of meditation, which are certainly also quite helpful, can simply not pass as authentically Christian unless they ultimately issue in a continually more "un-complicated" partaking and understanding of the Word of God and lead, in turn, to more willing obedience in living one's life accordingly. Otherwise—contrary to all the best intentions—the precious "pearls" of the Gospel, which one has perhaps come to know only as lusterless and dusted-over, will end up being exchanged for the fascinating gleam of unfamiliar meditative ways based on a taste for deep experience. This "discernment of spirits" —often conducive to misunderstanding on both sides— already points toward a second positional option in von Balthasar's interpretation of the creed:

Love rather than gnosis. Anyone looking for topical allusions to present-day historico-cultural and ecclesiastical questions in these meditations will, at first sight, not be able to find much; apart from the brief section on Jesus' birth of the Virgin Mary ("Here we have a great theater of war," 47), the entire exposition seems to unfold on the plane of a timelessly valid spiritual loftiness, and to be aimed at the eternal truths of faith. But this appearance is deceptive. Upon closer scrutiny, and after extended meditation, it becomes clear just how this way of understanding the Christian faith amounts to one great rejection of gnosticism, which has returned today with a vengeance and left its stamp on the mentality of so-called postmodernism. Gnosticism, that redemptive religion of late antiquity in the Roman Empire, which arose parallel to Christianity and developed in mutually defining interaction with it, has remained up until today *the* great temptation for precisely the pious and "inward-directed" among Christians. For, in a radical turning away from this evil world and history, it seeks redemption primarily in religious experience, by journeying inward with a view to discovering, in the depths of one's own soul, the "divine," through which God, humanity, and world are united with each other most deeply, that is, as grounded in "nature." Today, too, in the form of a new pantheistic mysticism of nature and cosmos that hopes to find, through the most varying modes of meditation and self-experience, ultimate redemption from the disastrous social and personal experiences of the present, gnosticism once again shapes the consciousness of many contemporaries, particularly of Christians.

To be sure, von Balthasar only seldom enters into this explicitly in his exposition of the creed; he also refrains from any acerbity or polemics against such historico-cultural trends, which had actually been worrying him for many years. At most, a few allusions are made to this contemporary temptation for Christianity: Such as, when he dissociates God's almightiness from the misapprehension that it is something "darkly elemental, eruptive, prelogical" (31); or when he rejects the notion that we can "characterize" ourselves "as part of God and thus ascribe necessity to ourselves" (37); or when he defends Jesus' bodily birth of the Virgin Mary against all minimizing interpretations and understands it as an expression of that "fruitfulness of virginal life... not toward regenerated mortality but into life everlasting" which was bestowed in the New Covenant and through which body and sex also take on "a new meaningfulness" (48); or when he insists on the corporeality and historicality of Jesus' Resurrection (57); or when, in the case of the penultimate article of faith, he does not speak—in the way usual in German renderings of the creed today—of a "resurrection of the dead," but consciously adheres to "resurrection of the body," and takes a decisive stand against a "bodiless soul" and the possibility of "reincarnation" (95). But all this still does not constitute the antignostic force that the text possesses for our times. That is grounded much more in the theological approach and characteristic tenor of the exposition as a whole: Not the "natural unity" between God, cosmos, and humanity is the sustaining ground and healing goal of our reality, but rather the "relational unity" between the Creator's love, which bestows itself freely upon the world, and creaturely love, which, in human beings, empowers a free response. A unity of this sort also preserves, even within the profoundest unification, the irremovable differences between God and world, humanity and nature, and self and other. The entire Christian faith rests upon this paradox: When love bestows *itself*, something *other* is allowed to be. What takes place fundamentally—that is, as "ground laying"—within the process of God's trinitarian love leaves its stamp upon the whole of created reality.

But today—in the face of depressing experiences of the fragility of all love relationships—precisely this insight is losing more and more of its credibility. In opposition to so threatening a decline in human and religious perceptive capacity, von Balthasar once again, in the present work, unflinchingly lays down his "credo": "Love alone is believable" (the title of a book that appeared in 1963 and contains, as if in condensed formulation, the whole of von Balthasar's thought); namely, the thing which is solely worthy of entrusting myself to, ultimately and comprehensively, in life and in death, is a love that can sustain and heal me in all situations. The Christian meets with this love in Jesus Christ; and when we have once come under the power of this "treasure" hidden in a field, we can really sell, with the lightest of hearts, everything else that the times have to offer, over and over again, as a means to salvation. This one love is enough for us, even if it often enough looks, when compared with the world's dazzling programs, like a paltry "mustard seed."

In view of this basic experience of belief, it becomes understandable why von Balthasar, a passionate advocate of the contemplative way of life, nevertheless (following Mt 25:31–46) regards *mercifulness* toward one's afflicted neighbor as the decisive criterion in the Last Judgment, and thus for our eternal salvation. In a very humanly touching way, this great speculative thinker responds to the question of what really holds valid in the end by referring quite simply to mercy: "Have we shown mercy, or only loved ourselves?" (70–71). It is in *accordance with this* that God's mercifulness will judge us, not in accordance with the height of our theological flights of mind, and also not in accordance with the depth of our mystical experiences of self and soul. Everything depends solely upon comprehending, as practiced in the communion of saints, the "height and depth of the love of Christ that surpasses all knowledge [*gnosis*]" (cf. Eph 3:18f.).

Insofar as contemplation and meditation help us toward this, they are Christianly integrated; otherwise, they remain susceptible to the gnostic temptation to self-redemption through self-experience. For even if the personal self may, in such experience, be expanded into cosmic-divine identity with everything, it nevertheless ultimately remains with itself. It is only arrival at something quite other than myself that first allows me to be freed from myself in such a way that I may live my life in the sphere of acceptance by the *other*. Whether I am actually serious about this desire to be freed from myself in the direction of God and his love, whether I really attempt, as determinedly as Jesus, to transcend the pleasant sphere of "birds of a feather flock together"— that is something for which mercifulness toward "others," who have fallen into need and irksomely cross and obstruct my path, remains a sound criterion running stubbornly counter to all (Christian or gnostic) wishes for spiritualization.

This view of the Christian path and goal corresponds precisely to those impressive words that von Balthasar formulated twenty-three years ago, when looking back over his previous work and ahead to its hoped-for completion:

"In the narrow span that remains to a sixty-year-old, neither images nor concepts are any longer decisive, but only the deed; for its sake, even the business of writing books will have to be buried; here, may God decree that not *only* what is paper molders away, but at least *one* grain of wheat might attain to the grace of resurrection! All paper is meant for the longer haul. What is important is not that something patient be printed, but that the impatient flesh be pressed and squeezed to see whether a few fruitful drops will perhaps ooze out of it. Squeezed it must be, if it is not to fail to pass through the small pathway, the narrow gate, and perhaps even the microscopic eye of the needle that, invisible to human sight, leads to the Kingdom" (*Rechenschaft*, Einsiedeln, 1965, p. 33).

That he himself was successful in this final passage through the narrow "eye of the needle" of judgment we may confidently hope, both for him and with him; for to the homecomer, this small gate simultaneously shows itself as the wide-open heart of the Son of Man.

Medard Kehl, S.J.

THE APOSTLES' CREED

I believe in God
the Father Almighty,
Creator of heaven and earth,
And in Jesus Christ,
His only Son our Lord,
who was conceived by the Holy Spirit,
born of the Virgin Mary,
suffered under Pontius Pilate,
was crucified, died, and was buried.
He descended into hell.
The third day
He arose again from the dead.
He ascended into heaven,
and sits at the right hand of God the Father Almighty.
From thence he shall come
to judge the living and the dead.
I believe in the Holy Spirit,
the holy, catholic Church,
the communion of saints,
the forgiveness of sins,
the resurrection of the body,
and life everlasting. Amen.

I

I BELIEVE IN
GOD THE FATHER ALMIGHTY

EVERYTHING manifold stems from something simple. The many parts of the human body, from the fertilized ovum. The twelve clauses of the Apostles' Creed, in the first instance, from the three component questions: Do you believe in God the Father, the Son, the Holy Spirit? But these three phrases, too, are an expression—and Jesus Christ provides the proof of this—of the fact that the one God is, in his essence, love and surrender. Jesus knows, and acknowledges, himself to be the Word, Son, expression, and self-surrender—bearing witness to itself in love—of that Origin prior to which no existent is thinkable and which he calls the "Father," who loves him and whom he loves in a common, divine Spirit of love, a Spirit whom he bestows upon us so that we can be drawn into this abyss of love (vast beyond measure) and thus comprehend something of its superabundance: "to know the love which surpasses knowledge" (Eph 3:19). Only with a constant view to this ground of unity, which discloses itself to us, too, is there any sense in unraveling the Christian creed: first, into the three leading strands already mentioned, which, in turn, wind out into the twelve "articles" (*articulus* means the joint holding the limbs together). We never believe in principles, but rather, in a single reality, which un-folds itself to us, for us, and in us, and is at the same time our highest truth and deepest salvation.

"I believe in God the Father Almighty, Creator of heaven and earth." Three statements about God: he is Father, Almighty, and Creator.

{ 1 }

THAT he is Father we know in utmost fullness from Jesus Christ, who constantly makes loving, thankful, and reverent reference to him as his Origin. It is because he bears fruit out of himself and requires no fructifying that he is called Father, and not in the sexual sense, for he will be the Creator of man and woman, and thus contains the primal qualities of woman in himself in the same simultaneously transcending way as those of man. (The Greek *gennad* can imply both siring and bearing, as can the word for to come into being: *ginomai*.) Jesus' words indicate that this fruitful self-surrender by the primal Origin has neither beginning nor end: It is a perpetual occurrence in which essence and activity coincide. Herein lies the most unfathomable aspect of the Mystery of God: that what is absolutely primal is no statically self-contained and comprehensible reality, but one that exists solely in dispensing itself: a flowing wellspring with no holding-trough beneath it, an act of procreation with no seminal vesicle, with no organism at all to perform the act. In the pure act of self-pouring-forth, God the Father is his self, or, if one wishes, a "person" (in a transcending way).

{ 2 }

When the New Testament refers to him in many passages as "almighty," it becomes evident from these that this almightiness can be none other than that of a surrender which is limited by nothing—what could surpass the power of bringing forth a God "equal in nature," that is, equally loving and equally powerful, not another God but an other in God ("In the beginning was the Word, and the Word was with God, and the Word was God," Jn 1:1)? If the act of creation is attributed later on to the almighty Father, the Gospel leaves no doubt that God the Son and the Holy Spirit take part with equal almightiness, but still with an almightiness that is originally grounded in the fatherly Origin. It is therefore essential, in the first instance, to see the unimaginable power of the Father in the force of his self-surrender, that is, of his love, and not, for example, in his being able to do this or that as he chooses. And it is just as essential not to understand the Father's love-almightiness as something darkly elemental, eruptive, prelogical, since his self-giving appears simultaneously as a self-thinking, self-stating, and self-expressing (Heb 1:3): The Logos, the Word that contains every sense in itself, is their product. Just as little is the Father's "all-mighty" self-testimony something compulsive; rather, it is also the origin of all freedom—once again, not in the sense of doing as one chooses, but in that of superior self-possession of the love which surrenders itself. This freedom is bestowed upon the Son along with divinity (he will become human in sovereign freedom and "call to him those whom he desires," Mk 3:13), and it is bestowed by both the Father and the Son upon the Holy Spirit, who "blows where he wills" (Jn 3:8).

{ 3 }

GOD'S LOVE is so complete in itself—he is lover, responding beloved, and union of the fruit of both—that he has need of no extradivine world in order to have something to love. If such a world is freely created by God, apart from any compelling need, then this occurs, from the viewpoint of the Father, in order to glorify the beloved Son; from the viewpoint of the loving Son, in order to lay everything as a gift at the Father's feet; and from the viewpoint of the Spirit, in order to lend new expression to the reciprocal love between Father and Son. Hence, the one triune God is Creator of the world. If this creation is attributed specifically to the Father, then that is because, within God, he is the Origin behind which nothing more can be sought.

Because, again, the work of the Son and the Spirit in the world is aimed at bringing all things home to this ultimate Origin, which has infinite room for everything ("In my Father's house are many rooms," Jn 14:2). And because, finally, the human spirit finds no rest until it has pressed forward to the starting point of all being and all love. Thus, too, there is talk of "heaven and earth," because the world, as the domicile of human beings, had always had an unreachable heaven above it—already in the ancient view of the world and much more so in the modern—in which connection this innerworldly unreachable is only a symbol for the "place" occupied by God in his creation, since it is impossible that he be absent from it. For "in him we live and move and have our being," therefore "seek him, in the hope that we might feel after him and find him" (Acts 17:27–28). To this end, his Word made flesh and his Spirit will assist us.

II

AND IN JESUS CHRIST,
HIS ONLY SON OUR LORD

THAT GOD is Father also means that he has a child. We transient creatures are not this child that God must have if he is to be called Father. There are billions of us, and none of us has a permanence that might be even remotely comparable to that of God. No, in order to be called Father, one who surrenders himself eternally, God must have a "single," "only begotten" Son. (We call him Son, and not Daughter, because he will appear in the world as male, and will do so in order to represent to us the authority of the fruitful fatherly Origin.) Christianity stands or falls with this assertion that there is an inner-divine fruitfulness (the Spirit will be named in the immediately following article), for if God is not in himself love, then, in order to be love, he would need the world, and that would spell the end of his divinity—or we would have to characterize ourselves as part of God and thus ascribe necessity to ourselves.

One may therefore say that Yahweh is a name for God that is still only on its way to the Father of Christ, and Allah such a name whose loving-kindness the Quran has taken over from the Bible. A God who is supposed to be love without being triune could possess only self-love; his need to love a world that is not himself remains, in the end, inexplicable. But now we Christians, too, must pose a question: Is a God who, as triune, exists as eternally self-surrendering love not also eternal enough unto himself? We have already called him Creator of heaven and earth, but why? Why does he want us, given that he does not need us and, with the world as it will be, is only burdening himself with endless troubles? Behaving, as

Saint Ignatius puts it in the concluding meditation of his *Exercises* (no. 236), "like someone carrying out a toilsome task"?

{ 2 }

IN OUR CREED, We speak of God's only Son as "Jesus Christ," which translates as "the messianically anointed Redeemer." We already give him the names that he received upon the occasion of his Incarnation. Is it thus really the case that, simultaneously with his eternal emergence out of the Father, this questionable, at once both magnificent and tragic world is also included in God's sight? It cannot be otherwise, for God has no ideas that "subsequently" occur to him. And yet we must distinguish, radically and unbridgeably, between the inner-divine emergence, which belongs to God's essence, and the world that was created on the basis of a free decision by the triune God. No matter how deeply God will initiate us, too, into his divine life, we will never pass from being creatures to being God. Why, then, is there a world at all?

As a Christian, one can venture an initial answer (nobody else can do so): If there must exist within God himself (in order that he can be called "love") a One and an Other and their Union, then it is "very good" that the Other exists, then the world is not, as in the rest of the monotheisms, a fall from the One. That is something, but by no means sufficient. And now matters become difficult, for if God decides to create free beings who can know and love him, he cannot "harden them in goodness" but must allow them (whether they be angels or human beings) the choice between the yes and the no. And what happens if, as is to be expected, they prefer the no? Naturally, God foresees from all time what he risks if he creates finite beings. The "Other" is, in the first instance, the Son, and therefore other beings can be created only in the Son ("without him was not anything made that was made," Jn 1:3). Hence, if the world is to be "risked" and judged conclusively to be "very good," it is the Son who is guarantor for the success of the venture. He is such all the more in that through this—concretely, through his Cross—he can demonstrate his infinite gratitude to the Father. And in doing precisely that, he will be allowed to prove to the creatures that God, despite all appearances, is the love that goes all the way "to the end" (Jn 13:1) of its possibilities.

Now, one must not imagine that God the Father, who was earlier described as "Creator of heaven and earth," forces, as it were, in the interest of accomplishing his plan for the world, the Son into becoming a human being and suffering. The Son and the Spirit are, after all, just as eternal as the Father, and the world is planned, in freedom, by the one, triune God. It was necessary that the world come into being in accordance with the archetype of the "Other," of the Son. And now, there is no other way to speak, in human terms, than to say: the Father entreats (as the first to do so!) the Son, under the supposition that creation of this world were to be successful, to act as guarantor for its salvation; in response to this entreaty, the Son entreats the Father, with a view to the latter's glorification (through Son and world together), to be allowed to undertake this work; and the Spirit's entreaty would then be that the mutual glorification of

Father and Son in the world might be completed through his sanctifying power.

Does all that explain the existence of the world? By no means in the sense that the world appears as something necessary. God's freedom, through which we exist, remains unfathomable, but we may, together with the Son, "our Lord," give thanks (*eucharistein*) to the triune God for our existence and salvation.

{ 3 }

"OUR LORD" we call the Son. "You call me Lord and Teacher, and you are right, for so I am" (Jn 13:13). When, as the risen Christ, he calls us his "brothers," that implies so great an honor that we, in accepting the appellation, acknowledge with Thomas more deeply than ever: "My Lord and my God." Precisely because he lowers himself so far as to wash our feet, precisely because he obliges lack of faith and allows his wounds to be touched. The term of address "Big Brother" we may best reserve for the Antichrist of Orwell or Solovyev. Nevertheless, he does not want us to be overcome with "fear of strangers" in his presence (as obviously happened to the disciples during the breakfast by the sea: "None of the disciples dared ask him, 'Who are you?' They knew it was the Lord," Jn 21:12). He wants us to stand beside him and to say the "Our Father" together with him. He wants something more: that we receive his forgiveness through confession and that we nourish ourselves on him eucharistically. It is *in* us that he wants to stand before the Father, indeed, *in* us that he wants to be in the Father. He wants us, the problematical creatures, to gain entry, having become in him "a new heaven and a new earth," into the inward life of divine love.

III

CONCEIVED BY THE HOLY SPIRIT, BORN OF THE VIRGIN MARY

"CONCEIVED." This is said of the Son of God, but it sounds passive; an Other is active in this conception, and he will be named immediately: the Holy Spirit. And an Other is she who conceives: the Virgin Mary. Just as a child is passive when conceived, whereas the parents take part actively. But it is only later on that a child awakens to consciousness, whereas the Son of God possesses eternal consciousness and also the will to become human. To be sure. Yet still we acknowledge in faith that he does not incarnate himself, does not himself take hold of the human nature that he will inhabit, but allows himself to be conveyed, as the "seed" of the Father, into the virginal womb by the Holy Spirit. But this means that the occasion of his Incarnation is already the beginning of his obedience. Theologians have very often claimed the opposite, on the ground that the union of the human and the divine natures occurs solely in the Son as the Second Person in the Divinity.

However, the creed describes not a "taking of something to oneself," but an "acquiescing in something that happens to one." In this pretemporal obedience, the Son still differs profoundly from naturally engendered human beings, who are not asked whether they wish to come into being or not; the Son permits, in full consciousness and with full consent to the divine plan for redemption, himself to be used as the Father wishes. But already here, he does so in the Holy Spirit of obedience, through which he will atone for the disobedience of Adam and "infiltrate" it. He does not, like a capitalist, cling to the treasure of his divinity as if he had earned it himself (Phil

2:6). He has received it from the Father and can "deposit" it with the Father in order to bring clearly to the fore, out of his eternal devotedness to the Father, the aspect of obedience that inheres in that devotedness and exemplifies what a creature should show in relation to God.

{ 2 }

"BY THE HOLY SPIRIT." He is the Spirit of the Father and of the Son. But now, when the Son becomes human, he, the indivisible Spirit of both, becomes, in the Father, the Spirit who issues directives and, in the Son, the Spirit who receives directives. Already so in the act of the Incarnation itself, since the Spirit conveys the Son, as "seed of the Father," into the Virgin's womb, and the Son, in the same Spirit, allows himself to be so conveyed. If the Holy Spirit, as a single Person, is both fruit of, and testimony to, the mutual love between Father and Son, then it is evident here how much the directing by the Father and the obeying by the incarnate Son are, right down to their deepest roots, consummate love. For us humans, that will mean that our obedience, which we owe to our Creator and Lord and to all his direct and indirect commands, can be, in Jesus Christ, and even must be, an expression of our love; so that any love of God or other human beings which excludes obedience, or wishes to get beyond it, does not at all deserve the name love.

{ 3 }

"BORN OF THE VIRGIN MARY." Here we have a great theater of war. If he is to become a human being, then why no normal human conception? And if this virginal birth (about which there was obviously no knowledge until relatively late; Paul still knows nothing of it, nor does Mark) is to be understood as an act of homage to a Jesus who is venerated as God, then must that not be connected with the influence of Hellenistic legends or rather more plausible Egyptian myths? And finally, even assuming that the (already married) Virgin could have conceived without male participation, are we to assume, even more improbably, that she also gave birth as a virgin? And is there not, by the way, ample talk of brothers of Jesus? So why make an exception solely for the "first-born" (Lk 2:7)?

A whole host of questions, which would require a book to answer. Here only in shorthand: the Virgin Birth stems directly from the early stages of the Old Covenant, when God restores sexual power to a waning body (Abraham, Zechariah and his barren wife), and the miracle that the "barren" woman will have more children than the fertile one is a stock symbol of God's power to reverse things. That is most likely the reason why the prophecy of Isaiah ("the young woman [or: virgin] shall bear," 7:14) is resolutely translated by "virgin" already in pre-Christian times (Septuagint). "Brothers" is used today, among many Arabic peoples, as a term for more distant relatives; this undoubtedly lies in the background to the Greek *adelphos*, which implies, in the narrower sense, "brother." And how typical of our age of minimalistic faith is the conceding of a virginal conception while dispensing the believer from having to accept a virginal birth. As if the second would not be as easy for God to bring about as the first. But then why? Because in the New Covenant the fruitfulness of virginal life (consider above all the Eucharist of Jesus), a fruitfulness not toward regenerated mortality but into life everlasting, will be a decisive feature of the new meaningfulness of body and sex.

To be noted well: this is not to deny to Mary the (messianic) pains, spiritual and physical, of her Advent— they represent solidarity with the chosen people and, in an anticipatory way, with the body of her Son (cf. Rev 12:2); but at Christmas, the Old Covenant and its expectations pass over into the quite different fulfillment of the New. All this is pure biblical logic, and all parallels with antiquity are lacking in the decisive depth that pertains to revelation.

IV

SUFFERED UNDER
PONTIUS PILATE,
DIED AND WAS BURIED,
DESCENDED INTO HELL

"Suffered." That the creed reports nothing about Jesus' public life, his teaching, his miracles, his gathering of disciples with a view to a future Church, is significant. It shows that Jesus' whole life and work was consciously understood by him himself as directed toward the coming "hour," at which—after a practical fiasco—the deciding act, which would turn everything around, would first be carried out: his suffering for the sinful, God-resisting world. It strikes me as rash to want to deny that Jesus made any direct, or indirect, predictions of his suffering, as if he had not known the ultimate reason for his having been sent into this world, as if his sharp rebuke to Peter ("you Satan," Mt 16:23), his directive to bear one's own cross daily and follow after him (Lk 14:27), his anxious longing for the "baptism" that he has to go through (Lk 12:50), were nothing but inventions of the early Church—not to mention Paul's theology of the Cross.

That Jesus did not have many of the details of the Passion before his eyes in advance, despite knowledge of them being attributed to him by the evangelists, need not be disputed, precisely because he left completely to the Father the entire arranging of the time and content of the "hour" (Mk 13:32). It is also not true that, through constant anticipation of the Cross, Jesus suffered continually in advance; he accepted unreservedly every gift from the Father, including that of joy, of sociability, of being allowed to confer benefits.

But the "hour and the power of darkness" (Lk 22:53), in which every kind of spiritual and physical suffering was inflicted upon him by men, and when even the Father abandoned the tormented one as well, is for us an unfathomable night. No meditation on the Stations of the Cross, not even the horrors of human torturings and concentration camps, can give us a picture of it. What it means to bear the burden of the world's guilt, to experience in oneself the inner perversion of a humankind that refuses any sort of service, any sort of respect, to God, and to do so in view of a God who turns away from these abominations—who can conceive of it? And as all those unsurveyable epochs, from the beginning to the end of the world, are brought together here, the Cross becomes timeless for the sufferer; there is no longer any question of looking ahead to the Resurrection on the day after tomorrow. The sinner can have hope, "sin" cannot; but for our sake, Christ was "made to be sin" (2 Cor 5:21).

{ 2 }

"DIED AND WAS BURIED." Died with the question to his vanished God as to why he had forsaken him, died with the surrender of his Spirit into the hands of the absent, died with a loud cry, in which (according to Nicholas of Cusa) God's no longer articulatable Word reaches its culmination. Died a death in final companionship with all sinners, but a dark death; for which night is darker than the one that the forlorn God has known most intimately? "And was buried," a fact which Paul also stresses (1 Cor 15:4, thereby obviously pointing out indirectly that the Resurrected was no longer in the tomb), was truly dead (as proven by the Shroud of Turin, whose authenticity can no longer be doubted today),[1] and had thus concluded, like each one of us, his earthly destiny.

{ 3 }

"Descended into hell." Naturally, since "Death" is "followed by Hades" (Rev 6:8), regarding whose hopelessness the Psalms give us a realistic picture. It was as a humanly dead man that the Son descended to the dead, and not as a victorious living one with an Easter banner, such as is depicted in Eastern icons through an anticipatory projection of the Resurrection onto Holy Saturday. The Church has forbidden the singing of hallelujahs on this day. And yet this new dead man is different from all the rest. He has died purely from love, from divine-human love; indeed, his death was the supreme act of that love, and love is the most living thing that there is. Thus his really being dead—and that means the loss of any and every sort of contact with God and his fellow human beings (one might reread the Psalms on this)—is also an act of his most living love. Here, in the utmost loneliness, it is preached to the dead, indeed, even more: communicated (1 Pet 3:19). The redemptive act of the Cross was by no means intended solely for the living, but also includes in itself all those who have died before or after it. Since this love-death of our Lord, death has taken on a quite different meaning; it can become for us an expression of our purest and most living love, assuming that we take it as a conferred opportunity to give ourselves unreservedly into the hands of God. It is then not merely an atonement for everything that we failed to do, but, beyond that, an earning of grace for others to abandon their egoism and choose love as their innermost disposition.

From Holy Saturday onward, death becomes purification. On that day, the dead Lord opened up a way out of eternal forlornness and into heaven: the fire that purifies the dead toward greater love. Under the Old Covenant, that did not exist; for everyone, there was only Sheol, the place of being dead. Descending into this, Christ has thrown open the entranceway to the Father.

V

THE THIRD DAY AROSE AGAIN
FROM THE DEAD

"RAISED on the third day in accordance with the scriptures," says Paul (1 Cor 15:4), and he also claims to see in the Resurrection, which was expected by no one, a fulfillment of prophecy, while the evangelists attribute this prophecy to the Lord himself (Mk 10:34).[2]

Establishing that the all-controlling turning point occurred on a prespecified day shows that this turning point was strictly provided for, and also able to be substantiated by witnesses, just like everything that had happened in Jesus' mortal life. The dating here is just as important as that of the Passion under Pontius Pilate. The point in time at which Jesus' new, deathless life takes its departure from our mortal history is no sometime or other, but a now that can be established for this history, which continues to unfold afterward. Not as though anyone might have been able to experience, as an observer, this breaking out of death into life; it is an event in God's history alone, no different, as such, from the event of the Incarnation. Nevertheless, both of these—entry into and departure from—affect our human history. The women and the disciples will encounter the Risen even on that same day, whereas Elizabeth recognized the event of the Incarnation within a few days after it took place (Lk 1:42f.).

{ 2 }

THE RESURRECTION of the dead Lord is usually attributed by Scripture to God the Father and his almightiness. That is appropriate, since, after all, it was mainly in obedience to the divine Father that the Son carried out the triune redemptive decision. In the farewell speech reported by John, Jesus, who will glorify the Father's love for the world through his Cross, requests of the Father his own glorification, and this had already been granted to him (Jn 13:32; 12:28). The Father's almightiness, as demonstrated in his turning death into eternal life, is praised by Paul as immeasurably great (Eph 1:19f.). But since it was the Holy Spirit of the Father and Son who mediated the whole of the redemptive work between heaven and earth, the raising from the dead can also be attributed to him (together with the Father) (Rom 8:11). And if the notion seems strange to us that a dead man should raise himself to life, it may still be said that Jesus—whose death, as I noted, was the work of his most living love, a love that was at one with the Spirit of divine love—himself played a part in enabling the turn around in his situation. From then on, he lives "to God" (Rom 6:10); but had he not always been living to God? And if he "died to sin, once for all" (ibid.), had he not already done that through his life and suffering? The one triune God effects the work that is, and remains, the central thing in the whole of human history: Those who are by nature finite, and have fallen captive to decay because of having turned away from God, are presented, through the calling back of the One into eternal life, with the hope, indeed, the certainty, of following after him (1 Cor 15:21–22).

{ 3 }

"FROM THE DEAD." This would therefore not mean leaving the dead behind, but rather, gathering them up and taking them along, as is wonderfully described in sermons of the Church fathers (see the homily in the Office for Holy Saturday). But when Paul then exclaims triumphantly, "O death, where is thy sting?" and "Death is swallowed up in victory" (1 Cor 15:54f.), that means something more: The reality of dying, as the human being's giving up of self—this reality has lost its sting (the feeling that, in the end, "it was all for nothing") and is drawn up into the process of eternal life. When the Father surrenders himself unreservedly to the Son, and when, in turn, the Father and Son surrender themselves similarly to the Holy Spirit, do we not find here the archetype of the most beautiful dying in the midst of eternal life? Is this final state of "not wanting to be for oneself" not precisely the prerequisite for the most blessed life? Into this most living "higher dying" our own wretched dying is taken up and resolved, so that everything human—its being saved, its living, its dying—is thenceforth securely integrated into a life that no longer knows any limits.

VI

ASCENDED INTO HEAVEN, HE SITS AT THE RIGHT HAND OF GOD ALMIGHTY

{ 1 }

THAT Jesus, the Resurrected, "ascended into heaven" does not imply a geographical event, but rather a return to the starting point of his mission, now laden, however, with the whole harvest of the world that he reaped through that mission. That what is involved here is not a change of place is evident just from the variety of relevant aspects recounted in Scripture. When Jesus appears to the weeping Magdalene and does not allow her to touch him because he has not yet ascended to the Father, he obviously wishes to let her share in his passage from the world of the dead into life everlasting: She is to give testimony about the happening itself to the disciples. When, at the end of the forty days, he appears visibly before the group of apostles, blessing them as he ascends toward heaven, that is in order to bring palpably before their eyes the fact that the mysterious period has ended during which, as an already heavenly being, he was completing his earthly work: He explains the Scripture to them, celebrates the Eucharist with them once again, finally selects Peter to be the shepherd of his flock, and promises that love, symbolized by John, will remain in the Church until his return. It would be senseless to apply chronological thinking here and to suppose that the union of the Resurrected with the Father could have taken place only after these days had ended.

{ 2 }

THAT THE Resurrected "sits at the right hand of God" is, of course, an image, and is intended to express the unprecedented elevation of human nature to the point of participation in the Father's majesty. The phrase "at the right hand" expresses the honor accorded it, as does the image of sitting. The dying Stephen sees "the Son of man standing at the right hand of God," which is expressive of the Exalted's readiness to act, as if he were about to take the one being stoned up to him. And Paul, who thrice recounts what he experienced on the way to Damascus (Acts 9; 22; 26), can hardly have seen Jesus sitting. He describes him elsewhere as "reigning until he has put all his enemies under his feet" (1 Cor 15:25), and the Book of Revelation depicts him at the moment of riding out to do battle against the anti-Christian powers (Rev 19:11–16). Thus it is true even of the Son of Man, who is fully perfect in himself, that he keeps on acting throughout the course of history until such time as "the world grows up into him who is the head, into Christ" (Eph 4:15). Thus the statement by the earthly Jesus that he does what he sees the Father doing (Jn 5:19f.) continues to hold true. In the life everlasting, resting and being active coincide: Only in that way is it actual life.

{ 3 }

THE EXALTED shares in the authority of the Almighty, for the Father "has given all judgment to the Son, that all may honor the Son, even as they honor the Father" (Jn 5:22f.). Which power could be greater than that of judging what is most intimate and most hidden in every human being and allocating to him or her eternal destiny accordingly? Almightiness consists much less in that which human beings imagine it to be, namely, changing things in accordance with one's own will—Jesus proved, through his miracles, that he could do that, too—than in exerting an influence on the freedom of human hearts without overpowering them. Enticing forth from them, through the mysterious power of grace, their free assent to the truly good.

The Church fathers used to say that God's grace works not through force but through "persuasion" (*suasione*), in that it suggests the choice of the better and gives the weak human will the strength to assent to that out of its own conviction and strength. Up to what point the sinful will can continue to resist this inner force of conviction exerted by the good—perhaps to the very last?—is something for only the almighty Judge of all hearts to know. This judgment, about whose procedure and content we can assert nothing in advance, is the subject of the next article in our creed.

VII

FROM THENCE HE SHALL COME TO JUDGE THE LIVING AND THE DEAD

1

"FROM THENCE HE SHALL COME"; that means from the Father, who has raised the incarnate Son to sit at his right hand. Fundamentally, the Son always comes from the Father, that is his essence. He comes as the Word, the expression, the realized love-almightiness of the Father. This "from the Father" does not, of course, imply any physical place, for the place of the Father encompasses every worldly place. He is in every place and simultaneously above every place. So, too, the "from thence" of the Son who comes to judge implies no physical locality but is the expression of a substantial emanation bearing the undiminished authority of the fatherly Origin. Still, the Son will exercise his authority as the one who he is: the one sent forth by the Father for the salvation of the world, the one who "died for all, that those who live might live no longer for themselves but for him who for their sake died and was raised" (2 Cor 5:15). Because he has experienced the guiltiness of all on his own body and in his own spirit, he knows them all from the inside and requires no testimonies from others in order to pronounce his judgment. "From thence" therefore means not only from the Father, from whom he eternally emanates, in whose power in shares, and from whom he has received his mission in the world, but also from this mission, which afforded him knowledge of all the heights and depths of creation.

2

"TO JUDGE." According to the German word *urteilen*, judging means dividing things fundamentally into distinct parts; without a division between yes and no, there is no judgment. According to the German word *entscheiden*, judging means separating things out from each other; without a separation into right and left, there is no judgment. This process of dividing and separating is vividly represented for us in the great judgment scene in Matthew 25. And right now, in the world and its history, there is undoubtedly much that needs to be divided and separated if the truth about the whole and the particular is to come to light. Further, this judgment does not merely aim at establishing what really existed in secrecy, but beyond that, at opening up, through its verdict, the way into the coming, the eternal. We all stand under this judgment, except for the Mother of the Lord, in whom there is nothing to be separated out; thus the icons depict her as the intercessor next to her judging Son ("Pray for us sinners, now and at the hour of our death"). How the Lord will judge, no one knows in advance; he tells us just one thing, namely, what he will judge about: "I was hungry, and you gave me food (or you gave me no food)." Me, in the least of my brethren. Have we shown mercy, or only loved ourselves? Once the documents have been presented, there is no longer any need at all to pronounce the verdict: "I will condemn you out of your own mouth, you wicked servant!" (Lk 19:22). "Should not you have had mercy on your fellow servant, as I had mercy on you?" (Mt 18:33). "Judgment is without mercy to one who has shown no mercy; yet mercy triumphs over judgment" (Jas 2:13).

Where will we stand, left or right? From what we know of ourselves, we can assume: most probably, on both sides. Much in us will appear to us ourselves, and especially to the Judge, as worthy of damnation; it belongs in the fire. That not everything in us was reprehensible, that we have not, our whole life long, from childhood on, said only no to love, is something that we might hope for from the grace of the Judge. Should it be fully in vain that he "died for us"?

{ 3 }

"THE LIVING AND THE DEAD." The first Christians had hoped to experience at least part of the Last Judgment before they themselves died. Paul, in his early times, says so explicitly (1 Thess 4:17). We, in our late times, do not know whether, when the Judge appears, there will be, along with the countless dead, also living persons who do not need to die in order to come to judgment; it is hot probable that anyone attains entry into life with God apart from death. The Book of Revelation describes the Last Judgment as one pertaining to the dead: "The dead were judged... by what they had done. And the sea gave up the dead in it, Death and Hades gave up the dead in them" (20:12f.). Should we designate "the living" as those who will pass the test of judgment, and "the dead" as those in whom nothing worthy of life everlasting is to be found? Such an interpretation is far from the spirit of the biblical texts. Even if it is said to one Christian communion: "I know your works; you have the name of being alive, and you are dead. Awake, and strengthen what remains and is on the point of death" (Rev 3:1–2), what is thereby expressed is only an extreme warning: The "dead" communion can, if it wants to, "awake." Even to the other communion, which imagines itself to be rich and wise while it is actually blind and naked, it is said: "Those whom I love, I reprove and chasten" (Rev 3:19). Here we can almost speak of awakenings from the dead. In the end, what is left to all of us is a unity of fear and hope, an attempt to throw ourselves blindly into the arms of the Lord, who knows and loves us.

VIII

I BELIEVE IN THE HOLY SPIRIT

FROM THE very start, Christianity has believed in the Holy Spirit and his divinity. The sayings about the Spirit in the farewell speeches already state the most profound things about him; in the Synoptics, "the Spirit of God" (Mt 12:28) is sent down upon Jesus from heaven (Mk 1:10), who himself "will baptize with the Holy Spirit and with fire" (Lk 3:16); the Spirit of the Father will inspire the witnesses of Christ when they are brought to court (Mt 10:20). For the belief and liturgy of the early Church, the threefold baptismal formula (Mt 28:19) excluded all doubt. But theology, because of the Arian crisis, had to reclaim once again, in a conscious way, the divinity of the Holy Spirit. First Athanasius, and after him Basil, argued, injudicious and pioneering writings, for the Church's belief, not directly characterizing the Spirit as God, but pointing out that his activities in the world were understandable only on the basis of his divinity; and soon after that came the definition by the First Council of Constantinople, whose authority was then finally recognized by the Council of Chalcedon.

The most mysterious aspect of God—"you hear the sound of it, but you do not know whence it comes or whither it goes" (Jn 3:8)—can, it is true, be confirmed by statement as something existent but can never be captured in rigid concepts. It is indicative that the dispute between the Eastern and Western Churches about this Mystery was never settled.

{ 2 }

THAT THE Holy Spirit is God is signified in Latin by the little word *in (Credo in Spiritum)*, that is: I give myself over, in belief, into the sacred and healing Mystery of the Spirit. Surely not into an impersonal power, for there can be no such thing in God, but rather into an incomprehensible Someone, who is someone Other than the Father and the Son (Jn 14:16), and whose characteristic task will be to work in a divinely free way from within the humanly free spirit, revealing to our limited minds the depths of God that only he has explored: "We have received . . . the Spirit which is from God, that we might understand the gifts bestowed on us by God" (1 Cor 2:12). To him, the most delicate, vulnerable, and precious one in God, we must open ourselves up, without defensiveness, without thinking that we know better, without hardening ourselves, so that we may undergo initiation by him into the Mystery that God is love. Let us not imagine that we already know this ourselves! "In this is love, not that we loved God but that he loved us and sent his Son to be the expiation for our sins" (1 Jn 4:10). The Spirit alone teaches us this reversal of perspective, but through him we can really learn what, in his view, love is.

{ 3 }

THIS incomprehensibly free-working thing in God is called *pneuma*: breath, or wind, or storm-squall (as at the Pentecost); the Resurrected breathes him upon the disciples, and based on that his emergence from God—for lack of a better term—is called a spiration. Something that stems from his innermost being; for it is said of the Crucified that, in dying, he "gave up" his *pneuma*. And is God's innermost being not love, and is the Spirit not thus present everywhere that this innermost occurs? That leaves us facing a delicate question: Can we say—as Western theology in particular has so persistently taught—that the generation of the Son must be a cognitive act (for human beings must always first know before they can love) and that the mutual relationship between Father and Son only subsequently becomes one of the love that allows the Spirit to emerge? Is the original surrender of the Father not already love from the start, communicating itself and surrendering everything of its own? So that the Spirit—as the Orthodox stubbornly continue to hold—proceeds from the Father just as does the Son? Since Augustine, Western thought has always conceded that the Spirit proceeds *principaliter* from the Father, a term that can be translated as "principally" or "originally." But since the Father gives over to the Son the power of being God in its entirety, so certainly, too— as a gift from the Father—he returns to the Son, equally powerfully, the receiving Spirit of love. If we exclude from the divine life any sort of temporal before and after, it would have to be possible to reconcile the Eastern viewpoint with the Western: If the Father generates the Son in love, there is no moment at which the Son would not already also, in the same love, both be allowing himself to be generated and returning this love in the Holy Spirit; so that the Spirit would already, from the first, be flaring up as the flame of love between the two of them, thus being simultaneously both origin and result of that love.

It would be erroneous to project the difference between the sexes upon God, and to see in the Spirit the feminine, the "womb" in which generation occurs. The creaturely difference (the implications of which, among humankind, by no means exhaust the whole range of love) stems from the plan of the triune God. If one wishes to go further, then the feminine would best be sought in the Son, who, in dying, allows the Church to emerge from himself, and who, in the whole of his earthly existence, allowed himself to be led and "fertilized" by the Father; but in such a way that, at the same time, as a man, he represents the originally generative force of God in the world. And since the Son proceeds from the Father, the different sexes are, in the end, present in the latter in a "preternatural" way; it was for this reason that, in the Old Covenant, his love could also be described in terms of feminine qualities. In the end, however, this inner-worldly difference belongs entirely to the "image and likeness" of a God who, even in his love, is "more dissimilar than similar" (Fourth Lateran Council) to everything created.

IX

I BELIEVE IN
THE HOLY, CATHOLIC CHURCH,
THE COMMUNION OF SAINTS

THE ACKNOWLEDGEMENT of belief in the Father, Son, and Spirit is finished. What still follows is acknowledgment, in belief, of the redemptive work of the three divine Persons. Therefore, in the German formulation of the creed, the little word *an* (Latin: *in*, in the sense of giving oneself over, in belief, to the Father, Son, and Spirit) is omitted after *glaube* ("believe") from this point on; rather, we now acknowledge, in belief in this God, what he has done for us in grace.

His first gift is the Church. That she exists and is known is presupposed; the individual believer, who says "I believe" (not "we believe"), does so within this sacred community. What she is remains, since she is the work of the triune God, mysterious in many respects. *Ecclesia* means she who is "called out," and the beginning of this call was the choice of Israel to be a "kingdom of priests and a holy nation"; its supreme flower became the Mother of the incarnate Son who, beneath the Cross, bequeathed this Mother to his new "Israel of God" (Gal 6:16) as an archetypal model; the Spirit of the Pentecost completes this work and appoints the members of the communion to carry out Christ's missionary command everywhere in the world. The Church, permanently rooted in Israel, elevated through the Son's Eucharist to being his incarnate Bride, and qualified through the Spirit to give worthy answer, is definitely a structure of the triune God that brings creation to completion.

{ 2 }

SHE IS "holy" through the sanctification of the Spirit, who, in the third article, descended upon the unblemished Virgin, which is why, primarily on her account, the Church can be called *immaculata* (Eph 5:27). She is "catholic" because, preserving in herself the Mystery of the entire living truth of God, she is called to communicate it, through her world-wide mission, to all of creation. By no means is she a "holy" enclave within a profane, godless world, but rather the movement, initiated by God, to communicate perfect salvation—a gift from God that we can assist in bestowing—to "all nations" in the Spirit and destiny of Jesus Christ, in his "universal authority" and presence ("always, to the close of the age") (Mt 28:18–20). Communication is more than instruction ("teach them to observe all that I have commanded you"); it is a drawing into God's sanctifying power ("baptizing them") and, with that, into the obligation to live one's life in accordance with this gift of grace. That such a commission, even under girding with the "whole armor of God" (Eph. 6:11), will lead to a constant succession of dramatic events ("like sheep among wolves") is something that Christ foresees quite clearly and relates to those who are his ("that when their hour comes you may remember that I told you of them," Jn 16:4); the Book of Revelation depicts the battle that surges through world history with unrelenting realism. The Acts of the Apostles and Paul's life alone are a singular testimony to the fact that the Church's catholic mission always proves itself victorious only in persecution, failure, and martyrdom: "You see, I have [on the Cross] overcome the world" (Jn 16:33).

{ 3 }

THE CHURCH is "the communion of saints"—in German, "the communion of the holy." This expression signifies first those "holy things," including above all the Eucharist, around which the Church assembles for purposes of her salvation and catholic mission. But precisely for that reason, the transition to "communion of holy persons" follows as an immediate consequence. And out of both, we have a glimpse into the unfathomable Mystery that, because Jesus "died for all," no one may any longer live and die for self alone (2 Cor 5:14f.); but that, in loving selflessness, as much of the good as anyone possesses belongs to all, which gives rise to an unending exchange and circulation of blood between all the members of the ecclesiastical Body of Christ. And precisely those members who are designated, in an eminent sense, as "holy" are like open treasure-houses accessible to all, like flowing fountains at which everyone can drink. Nothing in the communion of saints is private, although every-thing is personal. But "persons," in the Christian sense, are just such as, in imitation of the divine-human Person Jesus, "no longer live for themselves" and also no longer die for themselves.

It is here that the catholic and missionary task of the Catholica first becomes visible in its ultimate essence; in every instance, she anticipates, in prayer, devotion, sacrifice, and death for her brethren, that which she brings them through her outward missionary work. The proof: "little" Thérèse, as the patron saint of all missions.

X

THE FORGIVENESS OF SINS

ON THE one hand, this principle of faith does not seem particularly significant, because we hardly still have any conception of what sin actually means; there is so much injustice in the world, personal, social—what difference does "forgiveness" make to all that? On the other hand, the principle seems almost incomprehensible to us: How should a crime, an atrocity, simply be blotted out, as if the matter had never taken place? Remission of punishment would be legally, also interhumanly, understandable; but this erasing of all guilt—as Christians obviously imagine it on the occasion of baptism or confession—who could conceive of that?

But is it really so difficult? Can a mother not forgive her badly behaved child in such a way that, for both of them, the incident no longer exists, has disappeared into forgetfulness? Can something similar not also happen, in another context, between individuals reconciling themselves with one another? The saying, "I can forgive him for it, but not forget it," is a foolish one, because it shows that the forgiveness was not complete.

In the Our Father, human forgiving, which we can understand, is indissolubly linked with our hope and plea that God might expunge our debts, too, from his account book. Not as if our human forgiving would compel God to forgive us as well—nevertheless, he cannot absolve guilt if we ourselves withhold pardon and are therefore also unable to receive it from God.

"Forgiveness of sins" is, again, a work of the triune God. "Father, forgive them," says the Son on the Cross. And the Father forgives because he sees how fully the Son forgives his debtors; and both pour the Spirit of Holiness into the sinner's icy heart so that it might melt and the love within it begin to flow.

{ 2 }

INDEED, what is meant here initially is baptism, that baptism which Jesus himself underwent in the Jordan and at which the Holy Spirit descended upon him. Since then, it has been effective "for forgiveness of sins," as the Nicene Creed affirms. Not automatically, but also not merely on the basis of repentance and the will of the recipient to begin a new life in faith, hope, and love; rather, in such a way that, without this conversion, this giving oneself over to God, the sacrament initiated by Jesus is not effective. For this is the case with all sacraments—the Eucharist was already mentioned, and confession is something like baptism made newly effective—they are acts of God in a person, when that person opens up to them and entrusts him or herself to them in faith. If a person believes in the miracle, then it is, within the order defined by Christ and the Church, granted to him or her. Always to the individual believer. One cannot baptize a people, absolve a people, but always, even when many are present together, just this particular person who, like the woman with an issue of blood, touches Christ's garment. In the Old Covenant, the people were the partner in the covenant, they fell away from God, they cried to him in affliction, they were pardoned and taken back. No longer anything of that sort where God, as a human being, encounters individual human beings.

"What do you want me to do for you?" "Lord, let me

receive my sight." "Simon, do you love me?" "You know that I love you." "Tend my sheep." Here, too, belongs the representative power, conferred at Easter, of forgiving sins in the authority of Christ. It is impossible that just somebody or other could say to someone else: I pardon your murder, your adultery, your apostasy. Even if the Church permits everyone to dispense emergency baptism, that is only because it has received authority from the Lord to bind and loose in his name.

{ 3 }

AND YET, without calling into question what has been said, the forgiveness of wrongs is required of every believer. It is only after mutual reconciliation that the performance of Christian worship is permitted (Mt 5:23f.; Mk 11:25). Through Christ's act of atonement, God the father wanted to effect the occurrence of his reconciliation with the world, and in fact, to do so by resolving the element of justice (which is present in all love) at the inner-trinitarian level (between himself and the loving Son in the Spirit who partakes of both). Thus he also wishes that, among believers, the wronged party should take the initiative toward reconciliation ("If your brother has something against you, go and be reconciled to him"). Only as reconciled are we members of Christ. Therefore the apostle demands that "we who are strong ought to bear with the failings of the weak" (Rom 15:1), knowing that God perhaps finds our feeling of superiority harder to endure than the shortcomings of the weak.

As Christians, after all, we no longer live merely alongside one another, but, since we are part of the body of Christ, also, in a sense, inside one another; and indeed, not only with a group, not only with a communion or church, but with all those for whom Christ surrendered himself, in expiation, for the forgiveness of sins. No one is excepted from this. Therefore, a Christian does not know the word "enemy."

XI

THE RESURRECTION OF THE BODY

PURISTS have removed the word "body" from the creed as not sufficiently proper, with the result that now, in the German version of this acknowledgement of life, reference is made four times to the "dead" or "death," and a fifth, to "died." [3] This death was, of course, as we have seen, the supreme act of life and love, and thus a victory over the "netherworld," a victory for the benefit of the embodied human being who is destined for eternal life. A bodiless soul is not a human being, and reincarnation would never be able to redeem us from entrapment in death. But this hope, insane in view of decay and the grave, and also contradictory to all experience, hangs on one fact: Christ's Resurrection, apart from which all Christian belief is "in vain" (1 Cor 15:14). "See my hands and my feet, that it is I myself; handle me, and see; for a spirit has not flesh and bones as you see that I have" (Lk 24:39). Just when this miracle will be performed for us mortals—to speculate on that is idle; for the way that events succeed one another in the transtemporal sphere after death is something that God alone knows. And about the how, even Paul can only stammer in images and symbols (1 Cor 15:35ff.).

It is enough that we have received the following on testimony: in the Easter stories, the Lord appears bodily, but no longer tied to the laws of our time and space, no longer at the mercy of his material semblance, but free to make himself recognizable or not at will. Our acknowledgement of the resurrection of the body hangs by the thread of this testimony, and yet this thread is a supremely strong rope: nothing can be less likely to have been

invented by men than this report. The disbelief of the
disciples at the "idle tale" of the women who claimed to
have seen the Lord (Lk 24:11) is completely normal, and
the realistic conclusion to Mark's Gospel speaks of Jesus as
having upbraided them three times "because they had not
believed those who saw him after he had risen" (16:14).

{ 2 }

IT IS ESSENTIAL that Jesus displays the marks of his
wounds: hands, feet, and in John (for the unbelieving
Thomas) also his side. And this he does by no means
simply in order to identify himself (the disciples at
Emmaus recognize him by something else: the breaking
of bread), but as proof that all earthly suffering will pass
with us to the other side and be transfigured into
luminous eternal life. No suffering was as deep, and none
has had so final a meaning, as the Cross of the Lord; in no
case can it be overtaken as something now past and
consigned to mere memory; pain as such, all human pain,
all the suffering of the world, manifests here its eternally
persisting meaning. How this transformation takes place,
as eternally valid, is best shown by the Mystery of the
Eucharist: "This is the cup, . . . my blood, which is
poured out for you and for many for the forgiveness of
sins." *Effundetur*, it says, as future. But this pouring out is
unique: at that time, today, and in eternity; already at that
time in a sort of timelessness, physical and bloody; an
event that remains, with respect to its inner content,
unsurpassable even in the transfiguration of eternal life.

What a hope for all earthly sufferers, who are usually
unable to find any meaning in their suffering! It remains

in God's keeping, and is, in God, in a mysterious way, fruitful.

And often we Christians think that we sense in the cruellest suffering, incomprehensible in earthly terms—Auschwitz—a mysterious nearness to the meaninglessness and hidden necessity of Christ's Cross. All the horrors of world history will never equal what, at Golgotha, was the abandonment of God by God, but they all are taken up into this and preserved there.

{ 3 }

BUT WE MAY GO one step further. Scripture speaks of a "new heaven and a new earth" (Rev 21:1). These will not, however, be another, second creation, but rather the transformation, brought about by God, of his one and only creation. Not only will humanity, which is something like the result or the sum total of the created world, be resurrected, but the created world, too, which was its precondition and, in a certain sense, its family tree, keeps pressing on, from within, toward its own perfection. The Letter to the Romans states this expressly: the whole of creation lies in travail, groaning and longing for redemption, it wants to be set free "from its bondage to decay," from "nothingness" and "futility," and looks for this toward the "glorious liberty of the children of God," who already "have the first fruits of the Spirit": the resurrection begins with human beings and draws that of the world after them. What is involved is expressly "the redemption of our bodies" (Rom 8:23); the materiality of nature will not dissipate into Spirit but rather will take on a new form beyond the reach of decay. God creates only one world. Human beings have spoilt the Creator's work, the Son has redeemed the old creation through his Cross, the Spirit has sanctified it. This one world will be enough for God in eternity, and for us, whom he has created, redeemed, and sanctified, this God will be enough.

XII

AND LIFE EVERLASTING.
AMEN.

WE BELIEVE in the life everlasting without being able to foresee what it will be. Many have grown so weary of this transient life, so glutted, that they wish for only one thing: to sleep, to sink into oblivion, no longer to have to go on living. Great religions promise us that we could, if we follow their directives, set ourselves free from having to live. Nature, in its infinitely slow process of development, obviously has a drive toward, and thirst for, constantly more highly organized life; but once having reached the level of consciousness, at which there seems to be nothing more left to strive for, the impulse turns back upon itself and becomes a drive toward death. All that effort was, in the end, not worthwhile.

And now the ultimate and highest thing that Christian belief is supposed to be able to hope for is eternal life. "I am the resurrection and the life." "I am the way, and the truth, and the life." "He who believes in me, though he die, yet shall he live." Being, being conscious, being a person—as things eternally worth striving for? Yes, assuming that we understand the word "eternal" as "divine," for in God being a person means surrender, love, and fruitfulness, and only in that way is God eternal life: as something which holds sway eternally in the process of giving of itself and being given to, of making blissful and being made blissful. The pure opposite of the boredom of an exitless being-for-oneself. No, essentially a being-above-and-beyond-oneself, with all the surprises and adventures that such an excursion promises. One need only think away all temporality, which infallibly brings every path to the attainment of some goal, and what then? In eternity, the departure is always "right now": Right now I generate a God who is my Son, right now I experience the unutterable miracle of originating from the Father and owing myself to him, right now the forces of our love collide and produce—O unhoped for miracle—the common Spirit of love as a third, as fruit and witness and eternal kindler of our love. And because this now is wholly a process, the opposite of a standing still, it is the most exciting thing that there is; just as, on earth, there are stirrings of love even before they pass over into knowledge, habit, and perhaps surfeit. "The resurrection and the life": just as resurrection implies an enormous reversal, from emptiness to fullness, only once and right now; so, too, does the life everlasting.

{ 2 }

FOR ANYONE who is permitted to step out of his or her own narrow and finalized life, and into this life of God's, it seems as if vast spaces are opened up before one, taking one's breath away. Spaces into which one could hurl oneself in uttermost freedom, and these spaces are themselves freedoms that entice our love, accept it, and respond to it. Who, while still here below, could penetrate to the ground of another freedom? Impossible! Thus, in the communion of saints in God, the adventures of creative, imaginative love are intensified beyond all counting. Life in God becomes an absolute miracle. Nothing is given in a concluding way, the act of giving goes on unfolding boundlessly. The heavenly are therefore always ready to help in cases of earthly need—certainly through eternal, perhaps also through temporal, gifts—so as to rekindle our courage to strive, despite everything, toward the life everlasting, and to grant us a foretaste of that which awaits us. And if we are given to suffer, deeper shafts are sunk in us than we thought we could contain, depths destined to become, in the life everlasting, reservoirs of greater happiness, wells still more productive. Wells that flow forth of themselves, gratis; for in the life everlasting, all is gratis. The words "without money," "for no payment," when it is a matter of God's gifts, run through the whole of the Bible (Is 55:1; Sir 51:25; Mt 10:8; Rev 21:6; 22:17). This "gratis" is the innermost essence of divine love, which has no other ground than itself; and by it, everything that exists in eternal life with God is determined. And precisely because this love is without any ground, its depths cannot be plumbed; one never gets to the bottom of it, it remains deeper than anything that can be grounded or "put into concepts." Hence, Paul quite accurately says: "Know the love . . . which surpasses knowledge," in order to "be filled with all the fullness of God" (Eph 3:19).

{ 3 }

WITH THAT, the creed reaches its endless end. All the individual statements dissolve into one other, because they were all—even as historical facts—but an expression of the life everlasting in the symbolic language of finitude. Everything transient is only a symbol. It resembles from a distance, since it points back to something that is permanent and in process as an event. The human being was created as an "image and likeness" and even in faith sees but "in a mirror dimly"; once having arrived at God, however, I will "understand fully, even as I have been fully understood" (1 Cor 13:12); namely, by virtue of that love which has, from all eternity, conceived and known me.

PRAYER FOR THE SPIRIT

"Pour into our hearts the sentiment of Your love,"
become Yourself a flowing current for us, for our own
current does not carry us all the way to You.

Be rainfall upon our parchedness, be a river through our
landscape, that it might find in You a defining middle
and a cause of its increasing and bearing fruit.

And should Your water bring forth blossoms and fruit in
us, then let us not regard these as our own sproutings
and produce, for they stem from You; and let us lay
them up in advance with You, adding to the store of
invisible goods that You can dispose of as You wish.

They are fruits from our land, but brought forth by You,
which are Yours to use for You or for us, or to reserve
for another who has nothing.[4]

NOTES

[1] It was only after the author's death that the result of the carbon 14 test was announced according to which the cloth bearing the image was determined to have originated in the period between 1260 and 1390.—Ed.

[2] For details see K. Lehmann, *Auferweckt am dritten Tag nach der Schrift: Früheste Christologie, Bekenntnisbildung und Schriftauslegung im Lichte von I Kor. 15, 3–5* , Quaestiones disputatae 38, 2d ed. rev. (Freiburg i. Br., 1969).

[3] The German phrase, at this point in the creed, is *Auferstehung der Toten*, "resurrection of the dead." The other reference to death missing in the English version of the creed is in the phrase *Reich des Todes*, "Kingdom of death," which in English is rendered by the word "hell": "He descended into hell."—Ed.

[4] Extract from "Gebet um den Geist," in Hans Urs von Balthasar, *Spiritus Creator: Skizzen zur Theologie* (Einsiedein, 1967), p. 474. This text is printed on the image of a skull.